Learn the ABCs
Pp
Warren Rylands
and Eric Doty
IN GOD WE TRUST
LIBERTY
2014
LIGHTBOX
openlightbox.com

Go to **www.openlightbox.com** and enter this book's unique code.

ACCESS CODE

LBXR5463

Lightbox is an all-inclusive digital solution for the teaching and learning of curriculum topics in an original, groundbreaking way. Lightbox is based on National Curriculum Standards.

OPTIMIZED FOR

- ✓ TABLETS
- ✓ WHITEBOARDS
- ✓ COMPUTERS
- ✓ AND MUCH MORE!

STANDARD FEATURES OF LIGHTBOX

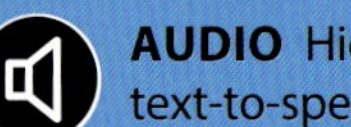

AUDIO High-quality narration using text-to-speech system

VIDEOS Embedded high-definition video clips

ACTIVITIES Printable PDFs that can be emailed and graded

WEBLINKS Curated links to external, child-safe resources

SLIDESHOWS Pictorial overviews of key concepts

INTERACTIVE MAPS Interactive maps and aerial satellite imagery

QUIZZES Ten multiple choice questions that are automatically graded and emailed for teacher assessment

KEY WORDS Matching key concepts to their definitions

VIDEOS

WEBLINKS

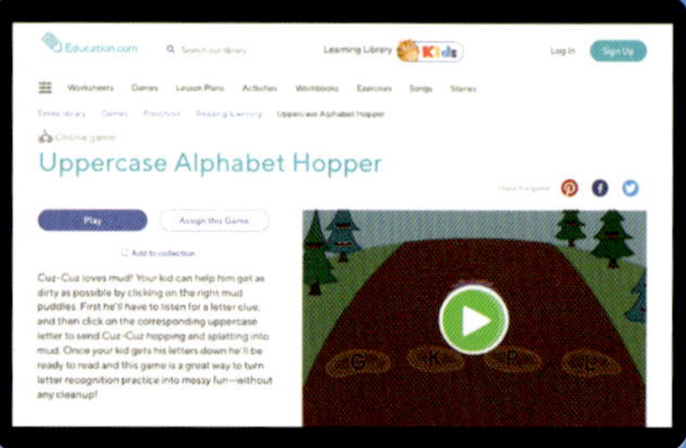

SLIDESHOWS

QUIZZES

This title is part of our Lightbox digital subscription

1-Year K–5 Subscription
ISBN 978-1-5105-5712-3

Access hundreds of Lightbox titles with our digital subscription. Sign up for a **FREE** subscription trial at **www.openlightbox.com/trial**

Pp

CONTENTS

Let's discover the letter

This is an uppercase P

This is how you write it

This is a lowercase 

This is how you write it

The letter p can start many words.

play

penny

peach

pizza

pelican

The letter p can be inside a word.

hippo

dolphin
apple
teepee
octopus

The letter p can be at the end of a word.

stamp

jeep

soap

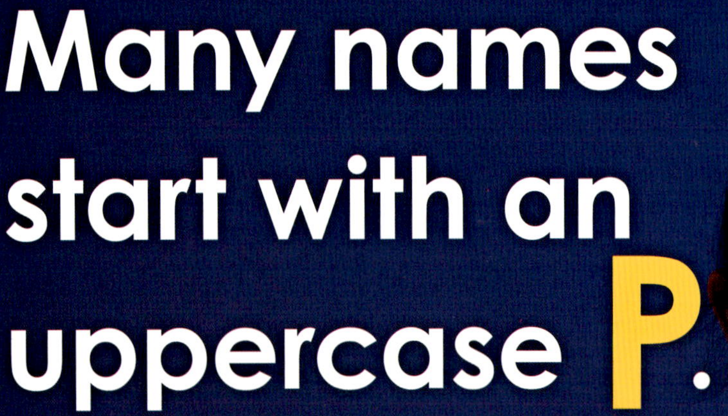

Many names start with an uppercase P.

Pat is happy.

Priyanka feels like dancing.

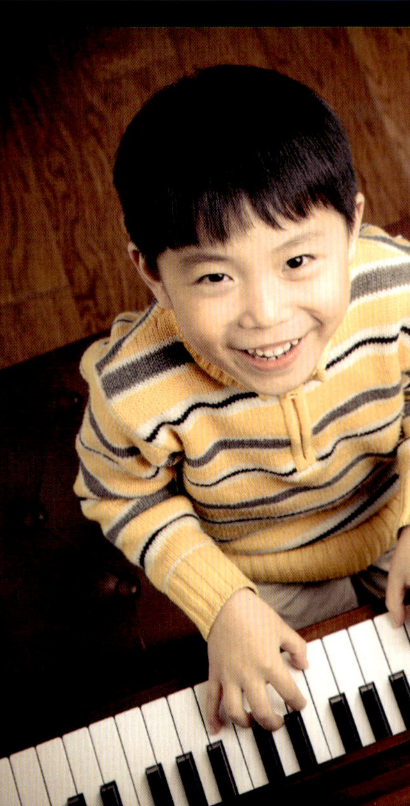

Paul can run fast.

Perry plays the piano.

Peter likes food.

The letter p makes different sounds.

pig

elephant

The letter p makes a p sound in the word pig.

The letter p makes an f sound in the word elephant.

The letter p makes a p sound in most words.

up
open
put
stop

The letter p makes an f sound when it comes before the letter h.

gopher

alphabet

photograph

nephew

Having Fun with P

Peter the panda had a penny. Purple soap costs two pennies.

Pam got paid for picking apples. Pam promised to mail Peter a penny.

She put a pink stamp on the package. The package came to Peter's teepee.

Finally, Peter could buy perfect purple soap!

The alphabet has 26 letters.

P is the sixteenth letter in the alphabet.

Aa Bb Cc Dd

Ee Ff Gg Hh Ii Jj

Kk Ll Mm Nn Oo

Pp Qq Rr Ss Tt Uu

Vv Ww Xx Yy Zz

KEY WORDS

Research has shown that as much as 65 percent of all written material published in English is made up of 300 words. These 300 words cannot be taught using pictures or learned by sounding them out. They must be recognized by sight. This book contains 47 common sight words to help young readers improve their reading fluency and comprehension. This book also teaches young readers several important content words, such as proper nouns. These words are paired with pictures to aid in learning and improve understanding.

Page	Sight Words First Appearance
4	let, letter, the
5	a, an, how, is, it, this, write, you
6	can, many, play, start, words
8	be
10	at, end, of
12	like, names, with
13	food, run
14	different, makes, sounds
15	in
16	most, people
17	open, put, stop, up
18	before, comes, when
20	for, had, got, two
21	came, could, on, she
22	has

Page	Content Words First Appearance
4	Pp
7	peach, pelican, penny, pizza
8	hippo
9	apple, dolphin, octopus, teepee
10	lollipop, sleep
11	jeep, soap, stamp
12	Pat, Priyanka
13	Paul, Perry, Peter, piano
14	elephant, pig
15	f
18	h, telephone
19	alphabet, gopher, nephew, photograph
20	apples, fun, Pam, panda
21	package

Published by Smartbook Media Inc.
276 5th Avenue, Suite 704 #917
New York, NY 10001
Website: www.openlightbox.com

Library of Congress Cataloging-in-Publication Data

Names: Rylands, Warren, author. | Doty, Eric, author.
Title: Pp / Warren Rylands and Eric Doty.
Description: New York, NY : Smartbook Media Inc,, [2022] | Series: Learn the ABCs | Audience: Grades K-1.
Identifiers: LCCN 2020054144 (print) | LCCN 2020054145 (ebook) | ISBN 9781510557802 (library binding) | ISBN 9781510557826 (ebook other)
Subjects: LCSH: English language--Consonants--Juvenile literature. | English literature--Alphabet--Juvenile literature.
Classification: LCC PE1165 .R9537 2022 (print) | LCC PE1165 (ebook) | DDC 428/.13--dc23
LC record available at https://lccn.loc.gov/2020054144
LC ebook record available at https://lccn.loc.gov/2020054145

Printed in Guangzhou, China
1 2 3 4 5 6 7 8 9 0 25 24 23 22 21

022021
110820

Art Director: Terry Paulhus **Project Coordinator:** Sara Cucini

The publisher acknowledges Getty Images as the primary image supplier for this title.